Magical Chants
Powerful Words for Every Day Use

LADY GIANNE

Introduction

Protection Chants

Healing Chants

Banishing Chants

Blessing Chants

Energy Chants

Money Chants

Love Chants

Wish Chants

Self Help Chants

Other Chants

Introduction

These chants can be chanted any time you feel the need. You can either speak the chant out loud or quietly in your head. The chant will work either way, it is just as strong chanted silently as it is spoken.

Chants can be used is a variety of ways. Many spells and rituals either require some language, or the caster feels adding some personal words would add to and strengthen their intent. Many practitioners have no problem coming up with their own chant while others need a bit of inspiration from time to time.

Any chant, prayer, or a particular verse that speaks to you is one you should take notice of so that it can be utilized later in your ritual work. If you are following a prewritten spell which provides you with a chant, you don't have to use it just because it's there. There may be another chant that you feel will be better suited to your needs. Go ahead and use it, personalization always adds to the power of your magic, it never takes away. Chants like the ones in this book can be used in your spell work, or used as inspiration for writing your own words. Add them to your magical repertoire and you will always have something to fall back on in any circumstance.

Chants can be used on the go. You don't need to be at your altar, or in your home, or somewhere private, performing a complex spell or ritual. With chanting, you carry magic with you that can be used in any situation no matter where you are. A chant is like a prayer or a meditation, it's always there in your mind, waiting to work for you.

You can chant or pray out loud if you wish, but your words will be just as strong if you simply repeat them in your head. You can gain as much from any prayer said silently as you would gain if one were spoken. This advantage gives you hidden power. In any situation, your magic is there for you to fall back on. Your favorite chants should always be memorized so you can use them anytime or anyplace.

You can repeat a chant as many times as you want, or simply say it once. If you are chanting for protection, keep repeating the chant until you feel safe. The same goes for raising energy. Chant your energizing words over and over until your energy is raised to the level you need.

For example, the Food Blessing chant:

Oh Mother Earth, we thank you so
For the food and beverage you bestow
For your protection and your love
And everything you do for us
We offer you thanks, love and mirth
As we eat your bounty, Mother Earth

This is likely to be said once. The blessing is complete. There is no need to repeat it; go ahead and start eating. Sometimes, a chant will be more powerful when repeated. For example,

Personal Space Protection:

Divine Goddess
If negativity dwells within this space
Make it leave, this is my personal place

This is more likely to be repeated. If you feel the need for protection, you probably do. If repeating the chant is increasing your sense of calm and well-being, by all means continue to repeat it as many times as needed. You will know when you are done.

To decide if a chant is right for you personally, speak the chant and also say it silently in your head. Repeat the chant with different emphasis and tone. You will know when you've got it the way you need it.

I speak through the dog
I chant through the
night
So mote it be
I know this is
right

✪ Protection Chants ✪

White Light Protection

While chanting, visualize three white rings surrounding
you. One ring around your head, another around your
center, and a third around your ankles:

Three times the rings go round
All evil shall stay on the ground
If any evil is near this place
It cannot enter my safety space
Three times three
So mote it be

Protection Against Worry

By the fire of my will
As I sit still
Protect my body, my mind, and my soul
Over which only I have control

Daily Protection Chant

Elements of Sun, elements of Day
Please watch over me as I make my way
In the morning light
I call upon you to keep me in your sight

Personal Space Protection

Divine Goddess
If negativity dwells within this space
Make it leave, this is my personal place

Protection at Night

Hail fair moon, ruler of the night
Watch over me, protect me, and keep me safe
Until dawn's early light

Pain Protection

Spirit of Fire
Through the light of your flame
Please take away all of my pain

Curse Protection

Turner be turned
Burner be burned
All that will find me is what is good
So that all may be as it should

Nightmare Protection

Go away evil dreams
I know you are not what you seem
Go away, stay far from my sight
So I can sleep through this blessed night

Basic Protection and Calming

I am peaceful, I am calm, and I am strong
The Goddess protects me harm, I am surrounded by her
arms

from

Personal Protection

Negativity is banished without a trace
It's gone from my space so I am safe
I am healthy, wise, and strong
Negativity will stay gone

Keep a Curse Away

A curse has been placed upon me
With intent to cause hurt
But it can't stick to me
I am protected you see
By the Lord and Lady and their hands on my head
The curse will be stopped, the curse will be dead

✪ Healing Chants ✪

Healing Chant

This spell I hereby intone
I am healthy from my skin to my bones

Spiritual Healing Chant

Healing rays come pouring in
Pain fades away for healing to begin
Divine love flows through me
Health and happiness comes to me
Healing the body, mind, and spirit
And as sure as the rising sun
Healthier daily do I thus become

Personal Healing

I heal my mind, my body, and my soul
I banish illness and take control
No sickness dares to stay in me
I speak these words to make it flee

For Good Health

Bring health to my body, and my soul too
Strength and well-being
Make it all new

✪ Banishing Chants ✪

Banish Negativity

Negativity
Leave me now, through the floor
You have no place here, I feel you no more

Stop the Evil Eye

I can feel that evil eye
You stare at me as I walk by
But I'm protected from above
By the God and Goddess and their love
You had better be careful of your negativity
And beware the power of three by three

Against Gossip

Your words cannot hurt me
And your thoughts I can't see
The Goddess will keep me safe from your harm
She holds me tightly in her arms

Banish Bad Thoughts

Bad thoughts, you have no hold
I'm banishing you to take control
All negative energy I now release
Allowing only thoughts that bring peace

Banish an Evil Spirit

Spirit, I feel you, and your power is bound
Back away from me, and stay on the ground
There you pass through the floor
Back where you came from, you are here no more

Chase Away Nightmares

Peaceful calming, restful sleep
Into which I fall deep
Nightmares banished out of my way
So I can rest, until the break of day

Banish Depression

Depression I banish you out of my head
Into a neutral place where you will be dead
And in the space you left behind
You leave me nothing to remind

✪ Blessing Chants ✪

Food Blessing

Oh Mother Earth, we thank you so
For the food and beverage you bestow
For your protection and your love
And everything you do for us
We offer you thanks, love and mirth
As we eat your bounty, Mother Earth

Garden Blessing

Holy Mother Earth, bless this garden, and the seeds we
sow
Bless them so they grow

Bedtime Blessing

In the comforting night,
That spreads like a blanket over your bed
The Goddess will protect you from fright
Her hand upon your very head

New Home Blessing

Goddess bless the mantel and the walls
Bless us here, where no negativity will fall
And any visitor who comes near
A three-fold blessing they will wear
Please bless my home that I will share

Energy Chants

Increase Creative Energy

Goddess Brigid, giver of the gift of creativity
Bestow your gifts on me
So that your energy will flow from me

Increase Creativity

Goddess Brigid, giver of creativity
Please let your gifts flow down to me
I need inspiration, I need it fast
Just enough to finish this task

Raise Personal Energy

O Goddess, I need your grace
To replenish my aura which has diminished in space
Hear my plea
So mote it be

Raise Personal Energy II

Eko, Eko, Azarak
Eko, Eko, Zomelak
Eko, Eko, Cernunnos
Eko, Eko, Aradia

Go to Sleep Chant

My quiet mind fills with calming peace
As I fall now into wonderful sleep
Nightmares keep far away
I will rest happily until the break of day

Stress Chant

I invite peace within me
And push stress away
So that with a calm mind
I can go about my day

Anxiety Chant

God and Goddess, please calm my head
Take away stress and anxiety, make them dead
Any negativity I now release
Instead I'm filled with calming peace

Confidence Chant

A clear head and a smart mind
I leave nerves behind
With good ideas and sharp eyes
Nothing will take me by surprise

The Call of Nine
Use this chant to call something to you.

With chant of one the spell's begun
With chant of two it will be true
With chant of three (insert what you are calling) come to me
With chant of four (insert what you are calling) flow through my door
With chant of five the spell is alive
With chant of six it is fixed
With chant of seven it falls to me from Heaven
With chant of eight this is what it takes
With chant of nine make (insert what you are calling) mine

Chant for a Productive Day

Goddess of Wisdom, I ask you to stay
As I go forth about my day
With ears open to hear and eyes open to see
As I will it, so mote it be

Increase Personal Energy

God and Goddess I respectfully ask
For increased energy to complete my task
By raising my energy I raise my power
My abilities and creativity increase for the next hour

Money Chants

Full Moon Money Chant

Money, money, money is for me
Money, money, money, come to me
Money, money, money is for me
I will tell nobody

Goddess Money Chant

O Goddess, inspire me
I call upon the money stream
Bring to me cash in reams
That I may have the riches I desire

Looking for Money

One coin here, another coin there
Prosperity is everywhere
I need some wealth, financial health
Just send me my share

Find a Job

I will get the job that I have earned
Using all of my experience and everything I've learned
It comes with respect and good pay
Steady work will come today

Attract Money

My hands are open, ready to hold
Wealth, jewels, silver and gold
Send to me a money stream
More than I've seen even in my dreams

Fast Money

Green brings me money, red brings me gold
Fast comes the cash, which I need to hold
My need is real, as you can see
Quickly money, come to me

Better Business Chant

I give my clients what they need
With a happy smile, I move with speed
I plan my work, and work my plan
Success and cash flow right to my hand

Love Chants

Looking for Love

Star of my love, burn so bright
I'm looking for true love tonight
Star of my love, show me the way
On the path of true love, don't lead me astray

Finding a Soul Mate

Lords of Karma, Ladies of Destiny
True love will now come to me
All the love that I send out
Will come back three by three
As it harms none, my will be done

Looking for a Lover

All the love that I send out
Shall multiply by three
I will find you, and you will love me with no doubt
So I will it, so mote it be

Fertility Chant

O Goddess, hear my plea
And send a baby to me
As I will it, so mote it be

To Heal a Relationship

Lovely Lady of the moon
I ask your help, I need it soon
Send your wisdom down to me
So that I may see where I have gone wrong
And how to be strong

Attract Love

I look for you, while you look for me
Open my eyes so that I can see
The way to the lover who lives in my heart
In his/her life I want to take part
All the love that I project comes back to me by three
As I will it, so mote it be

Finding Mr. Right

God and Goddess, I ask you to lead me to the one I know
is true
Please grant me your special sight
So that I may find my Mr. Right
Open my eyes so that I may find
That special man who was meant to be mine

Wish Chants

Basic Wish Chant

I call upon the powers that be
To bring what I want straight to me
By Fire, Air, Earth and Sea
As I do say, so mote it be

Wish Spell to Diana

You may do this chant this 3 times between new moons.
Go outside where you have a clear view of the moon.
Repeat 3 times:

Moon, moon, beautiful moon
Brighter than any star
Goddess of Light, Goddess of Love
Diana if it might be,
I pray bring fortune onto me
So I will it, so mote it be

Wishing Chant

Lord and Lady, I respectfully ask you
Please make this wish of mine come true
By the light of the sun and the power of the moon
Please grant me this boon

✴ Self Help Chants ✴

Stay on the Right Path

Lead me down the path of light
So that I may stay on the road that's right
Lord and Lady, show me the way
On my true track, I wish to stay

Make up your Mind

With my emotions stuck in a bind
I can't possibly make up my mind
Lord and Lady, please help me unwind
I need to decide, so send me a sign

Bring Good Luck

Acorns, bamboo, bats and black cats
Horseshoes, jade, and nautical stars
I call on you all to make my luck grow
Lend me your luck, let it flow

Social Confidence

I am happy, kind, and wise
I draw people like honey draws flies
I move with poise and grace
And banish doubt without a trace

Daily Prayer

As I start my day
I pray before going on my way
To be wise, confident and kind
And keep good thoughts in my mind
No matter what I might do
My intentions pure and heart is true
God and Goddess, please watch over me
So mote it be

Thankful Prayer

I am grateful for all that I have
Especially the good but also the bad
I feel blessed in many ways
Under the Lady's protecting gaze

Fear of Darkness

Lovely Lady of the moon, Ruler of the night
I call upon you take away my fright
And to keep my fears at bay
Until the bright light of the new day

For a Happy Home

Unhappiness I banish you from my home
Go and find some place to roam
We have no place for you here
And with these words you disappear

Make a Decision

God and Goddess, hear my plea
Open my eyes so that I may see
The right way out of this bind
With a good heart and clear mind

To Remember Dreams

I open my mind and its conscious streams
To help me remember in detail my dreams
And while my mind is open so wide
Only my dreams may come inside

Facing Fear

God and Goddess, lend me your ear
Give me the strength to face my fear
I want to stand proud and tall
With your support I can face anything at all

To Accept Change

Lord and Lady, open my eyes
Grant me your wisdom, make me wise
And strong to face what comes my way
Throughout this difficult day

Having a Bad Day

I am filled with calming peace
Which keeps my mind at ease
I will deal with whatever comes my way
Because I have the strength to get through today

Putting Today Behind You

Now I put this day behind me
And remember that everything bad will not always be
Tomorrow is a brand new day
And tomorrow things will go my way

Other Chants

Chant for Rain

Mother Earth, let the rain fall down
Giving life to the ground
Giving life to the seed
And a healthy harvest rain will bring

Chant to Call a Muse

Muse of Art, Muse of Sound
Take my thoughts and gather them round
I work beneath you in your guiding light
Please assist me in my creative rite

To Find a Lost Item

What is lost
Must be found
Since it's out of my sight
I ask for some light
Please show me the way
To the item I seek, this I pray

To Find a Lost Item II

Keeper of what disappears
Hear me now, open your ears
Find for me what I now seek
Open my eyes let me peek

To Find a Lost Item III

By the powers of moon, sun, Earth, air, fire, and sea
What now is lost shall return to me
So I will it, so mote it be

Find What Was Lost

Saint Anthony, help me find what I have lost
I've looked until my eyes are crossed
Lend me your eyes so that I may see
That which is remains hidden from me

Chant for Warmth

It is warmth that I desire
I wish to be near a warm fire
Its warming flames that I seek
I wish to gain some body heat

Chant for Coolness

It is cool which I desire
I wish to be a cold sapphire
A cool blowing wind with its chill
I want it be cold, it is my will

Chant to Pass a Test

On this test I take today
I will receive no less than an A
All my study comes back to me
Three by three, so mote it be

ALSO BY LADY GIANNE

Made in the USA
Columbia, SC
06 July 2022